Active Drama Playscripts

Teacher's Book
to accompany
Snow White
and
Murder Mystery Weekend

Contents

Introduction 2
- Why is drama beneficial in teaching literacy?
- Other literacy activities

Direction and rehearsal notes 4
- Warming up
- Speaking up
- Rehearsals
- Curtain call

The Plays 6

Snow White 6
- Props and costumes
- Scene notes

Murder Mystery Weekend 8
- Props and costumes
- Scene notes

Drama Games 10

Warm-up Games 10
- Scaring Your Partner
- Musical Statues Forfeit Game
- Mirror Exercise
- What Are You Doing?
- Me/You
- Throwing Words
- Name Game
- Stuck In The Mud
- Cat and Mouse Tiggy
- Human Knot
- Yes Let's Game
- Present Giving
- Props Game
- Wink Murder

Voice Games 12
- Group Speaking
- Zoom Screech
- Zip Zap Boing
- Adjective Name Game
- Juddering
- Front Of The Bus/Back Of The Bus
- Horse Blows
- Tongue Rolls
- Tongue Twisters

Rehearsal Games 13
- Sitting On The Chair
- Freeze As
- Slapstick Following Routine
- Walking Around The Room
- Get Into Groups Of
- Postcard Snapshot Scenes
- Before Aahh! And After
- Rewind
- Don't Bump Into The Table
- Mime Scenes
- KeyWord Stories
- One-Word Story
- Endings On A Piece Of Paper
- Mould A Shape Start A Scene

Introduction

The playscripts *Snow White*, a modern and humorous retelling of the traditional story, and *Murder Mystery Weekend*, an original detective play full of humour and suspense, have been written with Key Stage 2 pupils in mind, although both could be adapted for use with younger or older children. Young people have themselves contributed much to these final versions, so children should relate readily to the language and humour, and be involved in the drama process from the start.

Why is drama beneficial in teaching literacy?

Drama, and the examination of playscripts, help pupils get pace and accuracy into their reading. As actors, they develop listening skills as they wait for their cue, and learn to enjoy reading as they have fun exploring character through different ways of speaking. They will automatically start to develop the necessary skills to discover language for themselves as they learn to make sense of what they are saying through expression and intonation. Taking part in any performance, however informal, will help develop discipline and concentration.

Some of the drama games in this book can be used specifically to support word, sentence and text level work in the literacy hour:

Warm-up games (page 10)

- *Yes Let's* – helps to teach verbs (*running, jumping, skipping*)
- *What Are You Doing?* – helps to reinforce verbs and their use within a sentence (*I'm walking the dog*)
- *Throwing Words* – can be adapted to reinforce work on adjectives, nouns and verbs
- *Giving Presents* and *Props* – ideal for learning nouns, and can be extended to include adjectives (*a book/an old book*)

Voice games (page 12)

- *Group Speaking* – adds expression into speech, rather than reading 'parrot-fashion'.
- *Tongue Twisters* – ideal for reinforcing work on phonics. Comprehension also important – a tongue twister cannot be said successfully without understanding its meaning.
- *Adjective Name* – helps with learning adjectives, and with recognising initial letters and sounds (<u>W</u>acky <u>W</u>endy, <u>S</u>illy <u>S</u>amuel)

Rehearsal games (page 13)

- *Freeze As* and *Walking Around The Room* – although these games might not necessarily be appropriate within the literacy hour, they certainly reinforce word recognition work.

The following series of activities have a definite progression and are ideal for understanding the narrative structure of a story:

- *Postcard Snapshot Scenes* – this is the opening scene and step one in the process, defining character (who is in the scene?) and location (where are they?).
- *Before Aahh! and After* – the next step: adding drama (what has happened?). These frozen scenes are a great way to establish the beginning, middle and end (how did they deal with it?).
- *Slow-Motion Mime Scenes* – adding movement before words is a good way to develop the building blocks of storytelling.
- *Key Word Stories* – ideal for cutting out the 'little words' (*am, he, said*) and highlighting the main nouns, adjectives and verbs in the text.
- *One-Word Story* – a good listening game and a fun way to build a story. Can help with sentence structure and sense.

Other literacy activities

Playscripts are expected to be tackled every year throughout Key Stage 2. Obviously the emphasis and learning curve will be different in each year and the Active Drama Playscripts are designed to accommodate these various expectations. As a very broad example, while Year 3 are exploring character motives and writing their own 'whodunit' scripts, Year 4 could be rehearsing the entire *Murder Mystery Weekend* play. While Year 5 are directing each other in scenes from *Snow White* for dramatic performance, Year 6 could be exploring versions of the fairy tale from Brothers Grimm to Disney!

The playscripts can be used in a number of ways to support reading and writing work at text level.

Although individual scenes in both *Murder Mystery Weekend* and *Snow White* may only have a few speaking roles, repeating a scene with different readers can encourage pupils to experiment with voice and character by hearing other children's versions of the same scene. This will also help with varying reading levels, as any unfamiliar words will be read a number of times.

The playscripts can also be used to:

- discuss the features of a playscript and how it differs from a novel
- explore character
- prompt discussion about ways to portray the scene (the staging)
- explore the genre of a murder mystery/fairy tale
- play around with dialect. Try different accents with the characters
- rehearse/learn a scene.

Pupils can be asked to:

- write the play/chosen scene as a story.
- write their chosen character's history.
- write their own version of the fairy tale (*Snow White*).
- devise/plot a murder mystery.
- write their own play for classmates to perform (possibly scribe Postcard Snapshot Scenes – see page 14), using the same layout as the Active Drama Playscripts.
- describe/design scenery and how this helps the play as a whole
- list the clues from *Murder Mystery Weekend*
- explore the motives of each character in *Murder Mystery Weekend*
- write a props list.
- write the story in a different way eg: as a news bulletin.
- choose a character they would like to play and say why.
- write an epitaph for Snow White or Jill (the victim in *Murder Mystery Weekend*).
- write a synopsis of the play/chosen scene.

In the plenary at the end of the literacy hour, pupils could:

- Present/act out their short scenes to the class.
- stand as their chosen character and read their personal history.
- explain their set design.
- pass their written work to a classmate for them to read.

By passing their work on to another classmate, they are encouraged to make their writing legible and (hopefully) interesting. Often a competition for the best work, or, if doing script work, a presentation of a pupil's play by fellow classmates, can promote extra effort.

Direction and rehearsal notes

The playscripts can be used in a number of different ways outside the literacy hour: as a single play-reading lesson, giving every child a particular part or character; as a week-long project culminating in a low-key classroom performance, or as an end-of-term project, with weekly lessons devoted to rehearsing the script, exploring character and making props and costumes.

The following suggestions have come about from my own rehearsal sessions. Most are ideas the children have had themselves. There is no right or wrong in drama and the more input the children have in the actual process, the more they feel they are devising rather than being dictated to, the more spontaneous and fun the show will be.

One way of encouraging them is to join in yourself. Children love it when teachers get involved and although you don't always have their energy, if they see you enjoying yourself, they are more likely to abandon their inhibitions and produce good work.

I have also tried to cater for mixed abilities within the class. Some of the characters and scenes are more developed than others and there are a few words scattered throughout the scripts that they won't know. *Group Speaking* (page 12) will help children gain confidence with any words they don't recognise.

Warming up

Repetition is extremely important. Start each session in a circle with a basic warm-up game (see page 10). This allows you to focus the group and gauge their energy levels. Energy is the key to keeping momentum throughout the play, whether on-stage or waiting in the wings. A warm-up at the beginning of each lesson will also help get reluctant children moving!

Surprisingly, some of the more chaotic games are ideal in developing discipline. *Cat and Mouse Tiggy* is a good example – in this game, no matter how much they run around, very strict rules must be adhered to in order for the game to work. The same applies to *Walking Around The Room* and *Freeze As* – as soon as the signal is given, they MUST freeze.

Therefore, they are (hopefully) having fun, while learning stagecraft and gaining the necessary confidence to put on a show.

Speaking up

Why is it that children make so much noise everywhere but on stage? Put a script in front of them and they have voices like mice. Concentrating on a specific vocal warm-up will relax the jaw, isolate the tongue, wake up the face and above all, make them 'open their mouths'!

Although I have included many exercises to encourage and develop the voice, it is also important to remind children to:

- face the front
- not hide their face with their scripts
- stand up straight
- speak to the back of the room
- take big breaths
- keep their chin up
- make it loud!
- don't rush the lines (slow down and breathe)

Rehearsals

Most rehearsal sessions should not be longer than one hour. Devote the first 10 to 15 minutes to warm-up and voice games, and the rest of the lesson to script work. Concentration through a session can sometimes wane, so to keep their enthusiasm up, I often suggest a fun game to end the lesson – *Wink Murder* (page 12) is the most popular!

The Active Drama Playscripts have been written with the children's rehearsal process in mind. Most scenes only have two or three people in them, which allows for smaller group work and are flexible enough to incorporate any ideas the children may have.

After an initial read-through of the play, discuss the play as a class and ask what parts they would like to play. Before casting the play, allow them to workshop different scenes. This gives you a chance to see who would be most suitable in a particular role. However, you will never give everyone the part they want. Some will invariably be a character they don't like. Compromise and bribing techniques help immensely. Remind them that their ability to play a role does not just depend on how well they can act, but also how well they behave … if they play this part they don't like then later on they can play a part they do like. Give them the special task of understudying the role they want (this also helps if children are away).

The Key Stage 2 scripts are quite long, so you can also double up casts. I have suggested appropriate places to insert an interval in both *Snow White* and *Murder Mystery Weekend* and this would be an ideal time to do the change-over. This double casting is a great tool in rehearsals as each cast can perform their section of the play to the other half of the class. Both children playing a particular character can also work together on various character-building exercises, and so on.

Very often, Key Stage 2 pupils will be reluctant to put their scripts down, using them as a safety blanket. Make them do a run without scripts and prompt them as necessary. Very often they will be surprised at just how much they remember.

Further rehearsal lesson suggestions:

- in pairs, make up their own scenes based on the story
- break up into smaller groups and rehearse individual scenes from the play
- rehearse the same scene over and over in front of the group with different cast members each time
- do rehearsal games (page 13)
- do games for half the lesson and then pick up the scripts for the last half
- while working on a scene, rest of class are prop, costume, set making …
- do a speed run to help with pacing, tackle boredom, for fun, boldness of character. A time limit helps create a sense of urgency, unity and creativity.

Any groups that may be stuck or not working well can often be inspired into action by seeing the quality of work produced by other classmates. Performing helps the children gain confidence and it will train those watching into how to be a good audience, through listening, applauding and giving positive suggestions.

Some points for the children to remember:

- Just because they are not speaking does not mean they are not acting.
- Do not rush the lines.
- Pick up the cues. (This does not mean speak quickly, it means come in with your line straight after the other character finishes talking.)
- Physicality. Very often they become obsessed with words and forget about action. Remind them to act with their whole body, not just with their lines!
- Entrances and exits are so important and so easily forgotten. Entrances should be full of energy while ends of lines are often garbled in the rush to get off stage!
- Acting is reacting. Very often the children get so caught up with their own lines they forget to listen. This is particularly true with the Major's outbursts in *Murder Mystery Weekend*. Remind the children to react to them.
- It should be clear to us watching, *who* you are and *where* you are. Stay in character.
- The bolder and bigger the character, the less embarrassing it is.
- Learn how to 'hold your position' and don't fidget on stage.

Above all, though, the most important thing in any rehearsal is to encourage and guide the children's own ideas. Don't be afraid to play around with the scripts and add the children's suggestions.

Curtain call

At the end of the play it can be nice to do a curtain call. Get those children that have acted in particular scene or as a particular character to come forward, bow or curtsey and exit.

One idea is to top and tail the show with appropriate mood music. This music can be playing while the audience files in and played again at the end while actors leave the stage, particularly as the *Murder Mystery Weekend* cast is left frozen on-stage at the end!

The Plays

Snow White

This script makes an ideal end of term production. The most important thing, with a show this length, is to keep the pacing up – energy on entrances, snappy dialogue (particularly with the Dwarves) and big bold characters. Children must learn to listen for their cue lines and be patient while 'waiting in the wings'.

As most scenes have only two or three people in them, small groups can rehearse individually, before coming together as a whole. Although characters like the Journalist only appear once, there is nothing to stop them from re-appearing from time to time with a camera crew in tow, or doubling up as another character, such as the Pedlar Woman, one of the Forest Nasties or one of the Dwarves.

Although the following suggestions have been found to work in performing *Snow White*, allow your imagination (and the children's imagination) to add to and adapt the script. Past performances have had the Woods permanently on stage making up part of the scenery and parting only to allow people into the Dwarves' cottage, a split stage with the Dwarves' cottage on one side and the Evil Queen on the other, and a food fight finale involving members of the audience!

Props and costumes

The two main settings in *Snow White* are the castle, and the Dwarves' cottage hidden deep in the woods. The table and chairs for the Dwarves are not essential if staging size does not allow for them.

The Dwarves' costumes should reflect their names. Stinky, for example, can come on with an old banana peel on his head and dirt on his face while Tidy should be quite pristine. The only one who does not have a definite character is Fred. One idea is to have the Dwarves walking around on their knees (with shoes added for further effect) and Fred can then be normal size.

The Forest Nasties and Woods can be quite scary, dressed as trolls. They can wait in the wings and come on stage as necessary, or remain hidden amongst cardboard trees at the back of the stage until their appearances.

The Magic Mirror has many options (see page 10), but one of the most popular is to have a cardboard mirror frame or a box with an open TV screen which the actor can place over or in front of his/her head.

You will also need:

- red and blue ribbons, combs and brushes
- an apple
- birthday cake
- glasses, sunglasses, silly glasses for Nerdy
- dressing screen
- an axe
- sweater or jacket (for straitjacket)
- battle plan
- boots for Combat Snow White

Scene notes

Playscript: Act 1 scene 1 page 5

Narrator: The King, lonely without his wife, remarried.

At this point in the play, a frozen tableau of the wedding scene can suddenly materialise on the stage behind the Narrator and Interrupter, much like an illustration in a storybook. See *Postcard Snapshot Scenes* (page 14) to develop this idea. As the opening dialogue concludes, the scene can then fade, leaving the Evil Queen and Magic Mirror on stage to continue with the story.

Characters in this frozen tableau need not appear again or even be mentioned in the script, (for example, the King!) and to really extend the scene, whether in performance or as a rehearsal exercise, add music for the wedding march, basic dialogue (see *Key Word Stories*, page 16), dancing and frivolity.

✳

Playscript: Act 1 scene 2 page 5

Evil Queen: Mirror Mirror here I stand. Who's the fairest in the land?

Magic Mirror: Guess.

There are many staging ideas for these two characters. The Evil Queen can enter holding a vanity mirror, with the booming voice of the Magic Mirror coming through a backstage microphone.

There could be an empty box to one side of the stage, decorated to look like either a vanity mirror or a TV that gets switched on (see Props and Costumes, page 6), or the Magic Mirror could follow the Evil Queen on, mimicking her every move. See *Mirror Exercise*, page 10.

✳

> **Playscript: Act 1 scene 3 page 7**
>
> **Snow White:** I hope so.
>
> *Narrator enters and the action on stage freezes.*

This freezing idea is like the pause button on a video player. See *Freeze As* (page 13) and *Musical Statues Forfeit Game* (page 10) to help the children develop their 'freezing' skills.

> **Playscript: Act 1 scene 3 page 7**
>
> **Narrator:** *(Angry)* Will you stop changing the story. Let's go back to Snow White's entrance …
>
> *Narrator and Interrupter exit as the characters rewind.*

Again, like pressing the rewind button on the video player, the characters walk (and even talk) backwards until they are back in their initial positions ready to start the scene again. See *Rewind*, page 15.

✳

> **Playscript: Act 1 scene 4 page 9**
>
> **Snow White:** *(Calling)* Here, bunny bunny.
>
> *Snow White turns around and the Woodsman freezes so as not to be noticed. This creeping and freezing routine continues for a short time until Snow White eventually catches him.*

See *Slapstick Following Routine*, (page 14). The Woodsman is very often able to steal the show with this routine.

✳

> **Playscript: Act 1 scene 5 page 12**
>
> **Snow White:** Oh … Help!
>
> *Snow White gets chased by the Forest Nasties. Note: This chase is not confined to the stage …*

Snow White can be chased all through the audience, which is a good distraction if the stage needs to be re-set for the next scene at the Dwarves' cottage. You could add music to this chase sequence and although *Cat and Mouse Tiggy* (page 11) is a good grounding for this scene, it still needs to be choreographed for safety and timing. A whistle being blown, or a particular word being shouted is a good cue for the chase scene to end, for Snow White to make her way back on to the stage and for the play to commence.

> **Playscript: Act 1 scene 5 page 13**
>
> **Snow White:** *(To Forest Nasties who are unable to enter Dwarves' Cottage)* Ha, ha! You didn't get me.
>
> *Forest Nasties sulk off disappointed, followed by the Woods.*

The Forest Nasties don't have to exit, they can take up frozen positions on the side of the stage, signifying that the cottage is hidden deep in the menacing woods! *Freeze As* (page 13) and *Postcard Snapshot Scenes* (page 14) will help develop this staging idea.

✳

> **Playscript: Act 2 scene 2 page 20**
>
> *The real Snow White starts cleaning up the Dwarves' cottage on stage.*
>
> **Narrator:** … unaware that the Evil Queen was still plotting her death.
>
> **Interrupter:** So she did all that work for nothing? Typical.
>
> *Everyone exits.*

This is an alternative time to insert an interval. The first act of a play is often longer than the second and although an interval can be put almost anywhere, by putting it here, you can reorganise the stage and start with the Evil Queen and Magic Mirror for Act 2.

✳

> **Playscript: Act 2 scene 3 page 21**
>
> **Evil Queen:** *(From behind the screen.)* Oh I never have a thing to wear …
>
> *Pedlar Woman comes out from behind screen.*

The Pedlar Woman *is* a completely different person, not the Evil Queen, and is often played by a boy. A dressing screen can be used on stage to hide the other actor or the Evil Queen can exit, say her lines off-stage before the Pedlar Woman enters.

Murder Mystery Weekend

My aim in writing this was to get the children to explore the physicality of a character without the aid of costumes, using instead maybe one key prop or item of clothing. Although dressing up can certainly be great fun, I believe in starting with the basics and building from there. You create stronger characters and the costumes and props then aid the actors rather than clutter them with paraphernalia.

Most people in the play work in pairs (for example, Harold and Maude, Cook and Rival Cook). This means that pairs of actors can work together on their scenes, and will help to give each other confidence when it comes to performing on stage.

The second half of the play is performed around the table. Regardless of whether the play is performed on a stage or in-the-round, get the characters to stand when they speak. If they remain seated, their dialogue may get spoken into the table and be lost. This is also true of staging and movement. Open the action up. Get them to move away from the table and make sure they are not blocking other actors. A rough seating plan is shown below:

The main pieces of set in *Murder Mystery Weekend* are the table and chairs, and an armchair. The table can be covered with a cloth and dressed simply with cutlery and placemats. Try to avoid too much on the table such as centre pieces and candelabras. They get knocked over, forgotten or lost, or spend the whole show distracting from or blocking the actors.

As a simple costume idea, try giving each actor a very specific hat. These will suggest their character and can be a great device in hiding the murderer's identity!

Suggested hats:

- Jack wears a baseball cap as Repairman
- a turban for Madame Suzuki
- top hat for Harold
- a tiara for Maude
- pig tails and school hat for Jill
- policeman's helmet
- Sherlock Holmes hat for the Detective

Other props:

- place mats and cutlery
- place setting cards
- exclusive documents (for journalist)
- salt, pepper, and sugar pots
- magnifying glass (for detective)
- model film camera for Camera-Person

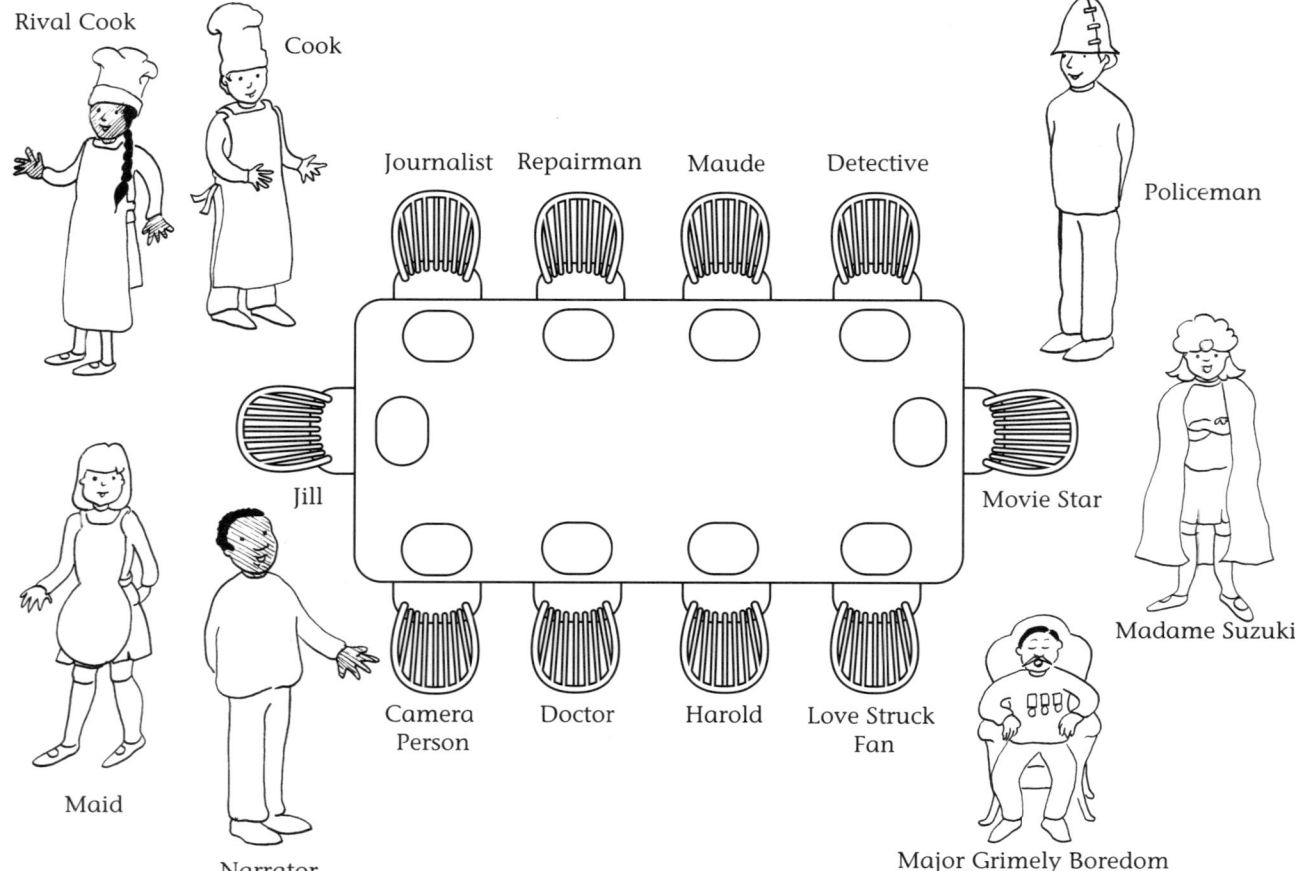

- notebook for journalist
- tool bag for Repairman
- model of small tape recorder for Doctor
- necklace

Scene notes

Playscript: Act 1 scene 1 page 3

Journalist:	I want a secret microphone under that chair there.
Major:	*(In his sleep)* Dinner!
Journalist:	Quiet!

The Major is technically asleep through such episodes. His outbursts should be both comical and surprising to the other actors (make sure they react physically). He should also aim to startle the audience before going back to sleep, eyes closed, snoring! See *Scaring Your Partner* (page 10) and *Zip Zap Boing* (page 12).

✳

Playscript: Act 1 scene 3 page 7

Doctor:	I'm staying for dinner too.
Major:	What?
Repairman:	*(Bangs head under the table)* OW!!
Doctor:	*(To Major)* What?
Major:	Good!

Again, pacing is important. This does not mean that lines are said quickly, but that there are not too many pauses between characters speaking. Sections such as this only work when the lines are performed quickly.

✳

Playscript: Act 1 scene 3 page 7

Repairman:	Job done! Chairs fixed! Hmm ... all that talk of dumplings has made me hungry.

Repairman pulls out a place setting for himself and puts it on the table.

Movements are important in this play, for example, the Repairman setting his place, and the Journalist and Camera-Person 'wiring up the room'. See *Mime Scenes* (page 15) to prevent the children blurring the action and rushing to get off-stage!

✳

Playscript: Act 1 scene 6 page 10

Everyone enters and takes their seat.

Jill:	Before we start, I'd like to introduce Madame Suzuki.
All:	*(Hello)*

This *(Hello)* should be in character and doesn't necessarily have to be the word *hello*! See *Walking Around The Room* (page 14) and *Sitting On The Chair* (page 13) exercises to prevent the children from coming in as themselves.

Playscript: Act 1 scene 6 page 11

Mme Suzuki: There will be a murder TONIGHT!

General GASP all round. Everyone then freezes in character.

This is often the best place for an interval, although the problem remains of getting the characters off-stage and then back on again for Act 2. Play some music while the cast silently exits. The process of moving between shots in *Before Aahh! And After* (page 15) can help to illustrate what is needed.

✳

Playscript: Act 1 scene 7 page 11

Mme Suzuki: Easy. I read the place settings. Now, could everyone please join hands? Concentrate.

Madame Suzuki does a (funny chant) that everyone copies ...

This can often be embarrassing and can result in a fit of giggles. Remind the children that the bigger and more silly they do it, the less embarrassing it is. Get them to copy you first. *Musical Statues Forfeit Game* will help with this scene, and with Jill's big dying scene (see below).

Playscript: Act 2 scene 1 page 12

Narrator: And then suddenly it happened ...

Narrator exits.

Big melodramatic dying scene from Jill. Rounds of applause from everyone.

For a bit of silliness, Jill can get up and take a bow at the end of her dying scene before lying back down dead again. As she is there for the rest of the play, one of the other characters could go and get her a cushion. Have fun with it!

Drama games

Although the following games have been categorised, there are obvious cross-overs. *Walking Around The Room*, for example, is shown as a Rehearsal Game but it is also great for warm-ups. Most of the activities have a natural progression and can be done in one session or broken up over the course of the rehearsal schedule.

Games are good because:

- they build confidence
- they stimulate thought and imagination
- they help develop character, fitness and voice

Warm-up Games

- Scaring Your Partner
- Musical Statues Forfeit Game
- Mirror Exercise
- What Are You Doing?
- Me/You
- Throwing Words
- Name Game
- Stuck In The Mud
- Cat and Mouse Tiggy
- Human Knot
- Yes Let's Game
- Present Giving
- Props Game
- Wink Murder

Scaring Your Partner

Two people sit looking at one another. While the rest of the group looks on, they take it in turns to try to scare each other. The aim is to get a reaction from your partner, for example, by shouting BOO and waving your arms in the air unexpectedly (physical contact is not allowed). If they succeed in getting a reaction (whether it's a laugh or a jolt) the person who reacted must leave and be replaced by someone else.

Musical Statues Forfeit Game

You will need a set of forfeit cards, a whistle, music or a very loud voice!

Music is played while the children walk around the space. When the music stops (or the whistle is blown) they must freeze or lie frozen flat on the floor. The last person to do so must take a card and perform the forfeit.

NB: Some children love getting caught out and have to be the centre of attention. Keep an eye and if necessary, change the way the game is structured, for example, instead of freezing they can play Pass The Parcel or Musical Chairs.

Suggested forfeits:

- do five push-ups
- tell the group one thing you like about yourself
- name three things that smell really bad
- do a belly dance
- act like a famous pop star
- with a partner, pretend to have a tennis match
- cluck like a chicken
- make the sounds of a racing car
- pat your head and rub your tummy
- do a big dying scene …

NB: Children are often embarrassed by having to perform forfeits, and end up in a fit of giggles. Remind them that it is less embarrassing, and more effective on stage, if they make their forfeit larger than life.

Mirror Exercise

Two people face each other. One person starts slowly moving while the other follows as the 'mirror image'. Eye contact must be kept the whole time, making the mirror use his/her peripheral vision. No giggling or sound is allowed, but facial expressions are, and if used, must be copied. Get children to explore levels (bending down, stretching up etc). Good for concentration.

What Are You Doing?

The group forms a circle with two people in the centre. Person A starts an action, eg: brushing teeth. Person B asks 'What are you doing?' and Person A must answer by describing a completely different action, for example, 'I'm mowing the lawn'. Person B starts mowing the lawn while Person A asks 'What are you doing?'. They continue swapping until one stalls or makes a mistake. He/she is replaced by another in the group until everyone has a turn.

NB: This is great for exploring levels. For example, if Person A is climbing a tree and has to think of something other than that, think low down, eg: tying a shoelace.

Me/You

In a circle, an invisible ball is thrown around the group. The person who throws says YOU and the person who catches says ME. Remind children you can throw a ball in different ways and that affects the way you catch it.

Throwing Words Game

A simple but fun game in which a word is thrown around the circle and the children have to react to the word thrown at them eg: slime, snake, muddy, doctor, windy etc. Children can move and use sound, but reactions should be short and fast – 10 or 20 seconds at the most. A good follow-on game from Me/You.

Name Game

Standing in a circle, someone starts by looking at someone else, saying his/her name and then walking slowly towards that person. The named person must then look at someone else, say his/her name and start walking before the first person reaches their spot. Once the children have got the hang of this game it can be speeded up and an elimination aspect added ie: if you are reached by your 'namer' before you've said someone else's name and moved, you're out. Ideal for concentration.

Stuck In The Mud

Great for developing team spirit. Someone is IT and has to get everyone else 'stuck in the mud'. If anyone is caught, he/she must stand frozen with legs apart and can only be saved if someone crawls through his/her legs. Watch out though! If the person saving gets caught before crawling all the way through, he/she is 'stuck in the mud' too.

Cat and Mouse Tiggy

This is an excellent warm-up game. A cat and a mouse are chosen. The other children make no less than four equal lines and position themselves like spokes in a wheel, facing the centre. The cat must chase the mouse and if the mouse is caught, they swap. In order to get away from the cat, the mouse may join the front of any line. This then makes the mouse 'safe' and turns the person on the back of that line into the mouse. The only major rule is that the cat and the mouse cannot cut through the lines.

NB: It is important that the lines remain straight. Every now and again, stop the action and reposition the 'spokes', leaving a central 'hole'.

Human Knot

This is ideal for ending a rehearsal session. Everyone bunches up with their arms high in the air. Every hand must hold a different hand. Without breaking the grip, the group un-knots itself. Can take two minutes or two hours, but it's always possible!

Yes Let's Game

The children stand in a circle. An activity is suggested by one person, for example: 'Let's skip'. The whole group then replies 'Yes Let's' and everyone then does that action. The next person in line then suggests another activity and everyone replies 'Yes Let's' before starting on the new action. It is imperative that the 'Yes Let's' be loud and said by the whole group. If the order in the line gets lost, just randomly point to people in the room. Remember the suggested activity should be non-verbal. As an alternative, suggest that anyone can call out at any time.

Suggestions:

- Let's ride a bike
- Let's go deep sea diving
- Let's join the circus
- Let's climb a ladder
- Let's fly a plane
- Let's play in a rock band
- Let's build a tree house
- Let's cut down a tree …

Present Giving

An invisible present is passed around the circle. Giving the present is just as important as receiving it. Remind the children to think of what they are actually giving – the weight, size, shape – and mime passing that object on. The person receiving it must say 'Thankyou, I've always wanted a ____' and name the present. Did they guess correctly? Were they close? Was it something similar in weight, size, shape?

Props Game

An ordinary object is passed around the circle and the children must use the object in any way other than its intended use. For example, a tea towel could become a skirt or a flying carpet; a wooden spoon could become a microphone or Pinnoccio's Nose …

Wink Murder

One person is the detective and is sent out of the room. The rest of the group close their eyes and the teacher chooses a 'murderer'. With the detective back, the group walks around the room and if the murderer winks at them they must die. The detective has three guesses to try and discover who the murderer is, while the murderer tries to kill everybody before being discovered.

Voice Games

- Group Speaking
- Zoom Screech
- Zip Zap Boing
- Adjective Name Game
- Juddering
- Front Of The Bus/Back Of The Bus
- Horse Blows
- Tongue Rolls
- Tongue Twisters

Group Speaking

This can help individual speakers overcome nerves as well as learn lines. To make sure the group speaks in time, pull out the key words of the piece and guide them with the rhythm. For example: 'Mirror Mirror here I stand … ' is a double time 4/4 beat. Get them to clap out the rhythm. Find other examples in the scripts where they could speak as a group. See what adding a comma or a full stop can do to the rhythm.

Zoom Screech

Start off by passing the word ZOOM around the circle. Speed it up and add action. Next, change the direction of the ZOOM by going SCREECH. The ZOOM must then go the other way. Experiment by sending the ZOOM across the circle. The only rule is, you can't SCREECH a SCREECH. Great fun if speeded up and actions are added.

NB: Children will quickly discover that the easy way out is to just keep saying SCREECH. Therefore, they may only say SCREECH three times in a row.

Zip Zap Boing

A more complicated version of *Zoom Screech* (above). A ZIP is passed around the circle. A ZAP is passed across the circle. A BOING sends the ZIP or the ZAP back to the person who sent it, who must then send it in a different direction or to a different person. The only rule is you can't BOING a BOING or say three BOINGs in a row! Add actions and eliminate those who make a mistake, and you will have a very popular game.

NB: If energy drops so does concentration. It is vital that movement to this game be big and loud and fast. Also a great warm-up game.

Adjective Name Game

Silly Sally, Wacky Wendy, Angry Andrew – with an action to match. Like the memory game above this also builds, with each child stating the previous child's name and doing the action, before adding their own. This is also a good warm-up game.

Juddering

This might also be called 'Shaking the sound out'. Start with the hand. Shake it and shake it and shake it, and on the count of three throw it across the room, letting your voice go with it. Do the same with the other hand, then arms, feet, legs. To finish, gently bounce/judder your whole body up and down letting the sound fall out. The jaw should be relaxed.

Front Of The Bus/Back Of The Bus

Generally pulling faces. Scrunch your face up as tight as it can go (front of the bus) and stretch it as wide as it can go (back of the bus). Add sound to it.

Ha (back) *Shoo* (front): ha shoo ha shoo ha shoo ha shoo. Continue with the sound *Ooo* (lips pursed) *Eee* (stretched): ooo eee ooo eee. Alternate between the two.

Horse Blows

Blowing air out, making the lips vibrate. The lips should be relaxed.

Tongue Rolls

With your lips closed, roll your tongue around the outside of your front teeth, 20 times clockwise, 20 times anti-clockwise. Judder your face to relax.

Tongue Twisters

- She makes a proper cup of coffee in a copper coffee pot.
- Rubber buggy bumpers.
- She sells seashells by the sea shore.
- Unique New York
- Watch the whacky wristwatch.
- Six thick thistle sticks.
- Black Rock Yacht Club
- Red Leather Yellow Leather
- Red Lorry Yellow Lorry

Peter Piper picked a peck of pickled pepper corns. A peck of pickled pepper corns Peter Piper picked. If Peter Piper picked a peck of pickled pepper corns, Where is that peck of pickled pepper corns Peter Piper picked?

Rehearsal Games

- Sitting On The Chair
- Freeze As
- Slapstick Following Routine
- Walking Around The Room
- Get Into Groups Of
- Postcard Snapshot Scenes
- Before Aahh! And After
- Rewind
- Don't Bump Into The Table
- Mime Scenes
- KeyWord Stories
- One-Word Story
- Endings On A Piece Of Paper
- Mould A Shape Start A Scene

Sitting On The Chair

A completely non-verbal game. With the rest of the group watching, one person must enter the space (as the specified character), take a seat (react to the specified scenario) and then exit. This is great for teaching concentration. Any fit of giggles or break in character and he/she must start again.

Suggested characters/scenarios:

- famous piano player entering the stage to play a concert, sits and then realises he/she's forgotten how to play …
- famous movie star/pop star coming in for a press conference, realises he/she has forgotten to put trousers/skirt on …
- spy sneaking into someone's office and sitting down at the computer to get some information before the boss comes back …
- young customer sneaking into a crowded cinema at the crucial point of the movie before realising it's the wrong movie …
- angry passenger grabbing the last seat on a crowded bus, before realising there's chewing gum on it …
- sitting at a restaurant, eating a big meal before sneaking out on the bill …
- enter excited, sit waiting for your date to turn up, they don't, leave disappointed …
- patient in a doctor's waiting room … etc

NB: Nine times out of ten, as soon as the children sit down they slouch. Ask them to freeze and point out how they are sitting before reminding them of how their character would sit.

Freeze As

The following exercise is designed to help develop the children's skill in freezing and holding that frozen position, as well as creating awareness of the space they are in.

As a group the children walk around the room. Call out a character, an emotion or an object and blow the whistle. Get them to freeze individually as that character, emotion or object. A great game to help develop their character.

NB: Very often they will clutter up in the middle, hide towards the back and hang around in pairs. Remind them to use the whole space, pointing out where they are in relation to others – they should not be touching (or talking!).

For example:

- an old person
- very scared
- cold
- as though you're under water
- a tree
- a policeman
- a robber
- a rabbit
- a gorilla
- a kung-fu expert
- a baby
- a weight-lifter
- a doctor
- their mum
- a super hero
- a librarian
- a teacher
- a witch …

NB: Point out exceptionally good freezes as it helps those without confidence and encourages extra effort in others.

Slapstick Following Routine

In pairs, one person must follow the other as closely as possible (much like a shadow). The person being followed can turn around at any time in an attempt to 'catch them out'. The 'shadow' must then freeze in the most ridiculous position possible. Do this game in front of an audience. It is hilarious to watch and great fun to do.

Suggested freezes:

- a lampshade
- karate expert
- a ballet dancer
- a tree

Walking Around The Room

The children must walk around the room, without talking or bumping into other children. When the whistle is blown (or hands are clapped) they must instantly change the direction they are walking in.

NB: Very often the group will automatically start walking in a circle. Break this cycle by getting them to freeze and pointing out where they are in relation to others. Suggest different ways of walking eg: not in a circle, speed up, slow down, walk backwards. Get them to explore silly walks.

Suggested variations:

- keep one person in view at all time (without this person knowing). Then two people, then three etc remind them they must keep walking.
- walking in the wind, rain, snow, mud etc.
- walking through knee-high water, waist high water, neck-high water …
- on the moon
- quietly tiptoeing so as not to wake anybody up
- in a mine field
- waving goodbye to someone
- walking as an old person, a fat person, their mother, father, brother etc …
- walking as each character from the play
- put a voice to your character eg: How would your character say hello? Greet other characters as your character.
- running for a bus
- trying to catch a long-lost friend
- trying to catch a bus that has a long-lost friend on it while running through snow (building basic scenarios)

NB: With the scenarios, voice can start to be added. Ask the children what they would say to get their friend's attention, to stop the bus from pulling away. Allow children to show their basic scenario to the rest of the class. This not only builds their confidence, but enthuses others with a performance energy.

Get Into Groups Of

This is a fabulous way to divide the whole group into smaller groups, and to trick the children into working with people they would not normally associate with. As they are 'walking around the room', call out a number, they must then create groups of that number. Variations on this can include an elimination of those children who weren't in a group of the correct number etc …

Postcard Snapshot Scenes

Instead of individual freezes, the whole group must work together to create a tableau scene or object. This exercise is well worth devoting an entire lesson to as you can progress from simple shapes, to complicated scenes. If necessary, the class can be divided into smaller groups and each asked to create their own tableau. The variations on a particular title are endless and it is often interesting to see how each group has interpreted each suggestion. Get the rest of the class to guess who each character is in each frozen tableau. Feel free to expand on the following guidelines.

NB: This is also a useful exercise for discovering the dynamics of a group, for example, who's bossy, who's quiet, who likes whom.

As a group create:

- the letter A
- a plus + sign
- an equals = sign
- a tree
- a hamburger
- a rollercoaster
- the beach
- a wedding
- the cinema
- school
- the park
- an enchanted forest …

NB: Try and get the group to advance to a stage where they can do this exercise without talking!

Before Aahh! And After

Using the scenes already suggested in Postcard Snapshot Scenes, the groups must come up with a set of three frozen scenes. The first sets up the scene (who, what, where). In the second something happens (an incident / accident / drama!) and by the third there is either the aftermath or conclusion. The audience can either close their eyes in-between scenes, or the group performing can move silently between each frozen shot.

Suggested scenes:

- at the graveyard
- the driving test
- learning to swim
- the maid vacuuming, finding necklace, working at Harold and Maude's (could also explore other character histories)

NB: Remind them to explore different levels. Not everything is done standing up!

Rewind

Exactly as the title suggests. The idea is to perform a short scene backwards. Experiment with speed, character and dialogue, and even walking backwards. As a follow-on from Before Aahh! And After (see above), get them to explore the frozen scenes in reverse.

Don't Bump Into The Table

A good memory and concentration game. One by one the children add an invisible object to the space. For example, the first person enters, applies lipstick in the mirror and exits. The next person enters, applies lipstick in the mirror and sets the table for dinner before leaving. Next person applies lipstick, sets the table and opens the door. They must try and keep the invisible objects in roughly the same position as they were. They can not just suddenly walk through the table that the previous person put there. Words or sentences can be added if necessary.

NB: If working with a large group, split them into smaller groups and then get each group to present their scene to the class. However, it can be fun to try and do one large scene.

Mime Scenes

No talking allowed – not even sound effects. Use facial expression and body movements only. In pairs the children must come up with a non-verbal scene to show to the rest of the group. It must be very clear to those watching *who* they are and *where* they are. Nothing really needs to happen at this stage, but if a story is developed, help them to shape it towards a natural conclusion.

Suggested locations:

- at a bus stop
- in a doctor's surgery
- at the beach
- at school
- on a pirate ship
- a disco
- in a supermarket
- taking a driving test
- on a film set
- at the gym
- robbing a bank
- putting a secret camera in the room …

NB: Try and get the children to come up with their own locations. Only suggest one if they are stuck.

Key Word Stories

A good follow-on from the *Mime Scenes*.
Allow each group to speak only the key words necessary for their scene. Get them to act each word as they say it. Ask the class for suggestions. There should be no little words or phrases in there, such as *I went, we said, now I* etc.

NB: Make sure everyone in the group gets to say something. Very often one person takes over the speaking while the others act. Divide appropriate words between the group eg: a giraffe at the zoo might say *Giraffe* while a monkey might say *Monkey* (or *banana* or both) – get them to explore words.

Key Word examples:

- door, locked, keys, lost, help, cold, hungry …
- zoo, excited, tickets, money, wow, giraffe, bear …
- class, teacher, dance, scared, nervous, step, kick, hurt, ow …
- police, quick, car, drive, chase, faster, faster, faster, stop …

One-Word Story

A topic or story title is given and the children, going around the circle, can only say one word each. The object is to make a coherent story. This is an ideal exercise to give everyone in the group a chance as no one child can force the story to go a particular way (although they try!). Encourages listening skills. It very often makes no sense, but that is half the fun. Try again with a new title.

Endings On A Piece Of Paper

A good narrative game and an ideal way to teach children how to finish a scene. Write down a selection of words or sentences. The children have to choose one and then make up a scene that ends with that particular word or sentence.

NB: Very often they hate their first choice. Allow them two choices and let them keep the best one.

Mould A Shape Start A Scene

In front of the rest of the class, two people stand up and each of them make a shape (that they can hold in a frozen position). The rest of the class then suggests *where* they could be, *what* they could be doing or *who* they are. They don't necessarily have to be people, they could be inanimate objects such as tables, sand castles, fountains, aeroplanes etc. Take as many suggestions as possible and when ready, get the two people on stage to choose one and perform a short scene.

NB: Whatever is suggested, needs to be related. For example, a ballet dancer and a racing car, although well suggested, need to be adapted so they can appear in the same scene together.